Salad

Salad

by Amy Nathan
Foreword by Barbara Tropp
Text by Kelly McCune and Amy Nathan
Photographs by Kathryn Kleinman
Chronicle Books, San Francisco
Printed in Japan.

Acknowledgments

This book represents the collaboration of many people.
We especially wish to thank:
·David Barich for all of his help in making this book possible.
·Kathy Hadley for her unending supply of garden greens.
·Jacqueline Jones for her design and ideas.
·Eloise Kleinman, Karen Kleinman, Rosemary Robertson,
  and Ellie Traugh for their contribution of wonderful plates
  and other essentials.
·Bob Lambert for his Cucumber Ice recipe, wonderful palate,
  and selfless collaboration.
·Barton Levenson for sharing her recipes for Wild Onion Antipasto,
  Wild and Gathered Greens, and Scented Geranium Vinaigrette.
·Patrice Lewandowski for her Future Salad, many inspirations,
  and salad thinking.
·Kit Morris for her photo assistance, her organization, and her support.
·Michael Schwab and Tom Ingalls for their love and support.
·Cindy Pawlcyn for her inspirational salad making.
·Sara Slavin for her beautiful plate and her support.
·Mark Steisel for his advice.
·Mary VanDamme for her exquisite handmade plates.
·Also special thanks to Susan de Vaty, Terri Driscoll,
  Edward Hughes-Gardiner and Laura Lamar.

Book and cover design by Jacqueline Jones
Art direction by Kathryn Kleinman and Amy Nathan
Photography by Kathryn Kleinman
Food styling by Amy Nathan
Edited by Carolyn Miller
Photography assistance by Kit Morris
Mechanical production by Mary Lynne Barbis, Susan Bard,
Terri Driscoll and Laurie Phillips,
Jacqueline Jones Design

Printed in Japan
by Dai Nippon Printing Company, Ltd., Tokyo, Japan

Library of Congress Cataloging in Publication Data:
Kleinman, Kathryn.
  Salad.
  Includes index.
  1. Salads. I. Nathan, Amy. II. Title.
TX740.K53   1985   641.8'3   84-28519
ISBN 0-87701-348-9
10 9 8 7 6 5

Distributed in Canada by
Raincoast Books
112 East 3rd Ave.
Vancouver, B.C.
V5T 1C8

Chronicle Books
One Hallidie Plaza
San Francisco
California 94102

Foreword

My remembrances of salad go no deeper than the wispy roots on a baby radish. A suburban child of the fifties growing up in the New Jersey nursery town of Springfield, salad to me was iceberg lettuce and 1890's French Dressing. I loved it, pure and simple. The crunch of the refrigerated, watery lettuce and the tang of the red syrup were perfectly delicious on my child's tongue. Salad *chez Tropp* was a glorious relief from the dinnertime boredom of lamb chops and mashed potatoes, and I lusted for it. I tried growing up in many ways—few of them culinary—and acquired some special adolescent salad passions en route. One was for the square foil packages of dry dressing you could shake up like confetti in a bottle filled with Wesson oil and cheap vinegar. Another was for the archetypal salad served in lesser New York pizza joints (and also a few disreputable places on the Jersey shore), the kind that featured a chilled jumble of paper-thin red onions and iceberg wedges heaped with some lumps of feta in imitation wooden bowls. Nonetheless, the pinnacle of the early salad years came one day in Taiwan, when, by imperious command of the old gastronome who headed my Chinese family, I bought a pouch each of ersatz mayonnaise and ketchup on Taipei's black market, whipped the mess into Russian dressing with chopsticks, and scooped it into rice bowls over chlorine-soaked lettuce as an "exotic" first course. By the time I moved body and wok to San Francisco I knew nothing further of the world of salad. It was then by sheer accident that Alice Waters appeared one day to take me to lunch. It was her day off, and Alice arrived wearing a Russian tunic in the battered Chez Panisse pick-up truck, empty of the usual mad-dash-before-dinner vegetables and filled instead with a big basket of wild flowers. Off we drove to Greens, the newly opened vegetarian restaurant on San Francisco Bay. There the flower basket was given to the chef, a Zen priestess named Deborah Madison who had trained in Panisse's kitchen, and Alice and I were seated for lunch. Lunch was a revelation. The only comparable memory I have is that of the first time I stumbled into the Museum of Modern Art in New York and stood astounded in front of a Rousseau jungle. Such was the feeling of a Salad Primitive sitting down to a meal of mysterious greens—some straight, some twisted, tasting variously sweet, bitter, cool and hot, garnished inexplicably and perhaps dangerously with furry branches and tiny blossoms. Was I to eat this? I did, and slipped down the rabbit hole. It was suddenly a world where potatoes were the size of marbles, vinegars and oils came in more than one flavor, and herbs set my nose twitching. Not much time passed before, drawn by Zen winds and the scent of salads, I was an apprentice in the kitchen at Greens. In the morning, I cleaned lettuces and chopped herbs—*mâche*, rocket, chicory, endive, sorrel and dandelion, basil, rosemary, chervil, tarragon, and chives—forever mixing the names. By late noon, vinaigrettes brought forth a rainbow of oils and vinegars, all to be tasted and balanced. And then at night I gamely tossed the tender leaves with dressing and occasional flowers to order, my hands dumb when compared to Deborah's, from whose fingers salads fell perfectly poised on their chilled plates. Now it is years later and I am salads wiser. Curiously, I rarely eat them these days, though I salute all the little lettuces and straight-standing herbs so regularly appearing in our markets. They steal seductively with their wonderful shapes and colors into even my very Chinese kitchen—red *radicchio* leaves to cradle Cantonese minced squab, tiny gourdlike golden tomatoes to enliven Peking cold noodles, or a shower of lavender chive blossoms to lend their pretty bitterness to a festive bowl of shrimp and pine nut fried rice. Shyly and happily, salads tip-toe through my dishes. How very strange it is then that this funny, half-salad person should be asked to pen a foreword to an extraordinary salad book. Once again, we have all slipped down the rabbit hole! Here is a veritable salad kaleidoscope, an ode to the Goddess Salad. Flip the pages, chase the shapes, eat the colors! It is a perfect homage to the Lords Lettuce and Tomato, decked before us in all their remarkable finery. I thank the caring authors. Each is an enchantress, and this book is an enchantment.

Barbara Tropp, San Francisco
Author, The Modern Art of Chinese Cooking.
Chef/Owner, CHINA MOON.

Introduction

In 1981 I tasted a salad that changed the course of all my salad making. Its flavors awakened my palate from spinach-salad slumber, and my eyes from the usual green toss. It contained ingredients I had never seen or tasted, such as tender mâche, sun-dried tomatoes, olive paste, and bufalo mozzarella. This was not a salad to stumble through to get to the main course; it was a participatory salad, for each new color, taste, and texture was to be arranged in small bites on a tangy Belgian endive spear. The tart and sweet ingredients combined to make a dozen flavor variations, and I was mesmerized. I tracked down the ingredients and created my own "New Italian Antipasto" salad. I later discovered that this wonderful salad had originated with Cindy Pawlcyn, chef and owner of Mustard's Grill in Napa. I was inspired. I began to experiment with new flavor combinations, to seek out new greens, and to bring more color, texture, and shape into play in my salads. Markets in the Bay Area were just beginning to offer a wider variety of salad ingredients and more unusual greens. The abundance of edible greens, herbs, and flowers growing in the countryside allowed my salad compositions to go in new directions. In restaurants, chefs were paying particular attention to salad. Since it was my favorite part of a meal, I was thrilled. Some salads were savory and substantial enough to be a meal in and of themselves. I drew inspiration from the "greats" such as Jeremiah Tower, Alice Waters, and Bruce LeFavour. I sought out restaurants serving innovative salads, such as Andalou and the New Boonville Hotel. Most of the salads I was enjoying were created around the French tradition of mesclun, a mixture of young, freshly picked lettuces, and other seasonal ingredients, both usual and unusual. I began to incorporate this combination in my own salad making. People responded. They inquired about my vinaigrettes, which to me were embarrassingly simple. They seemed to enjoy the visual delight of the compositions as well as the savory delight of the flavor combinations. This book grew out of those two principles: simplicity and inspiration. I do not spend a lot of time on preparation; I do spend a lot of time looking, planning, and selecting. Salad ingredients are some of the most beautiful edibles you will find, and a salad can be a touch of the garden brought indoors. Here are some guidelines for your own salad making. Begin with the highest-quality ingredients available to you, whether they come from the market, the garden, or your walk in the countryside. If you are marketing, decide what ingredients to purchase once you are there, not before. Choose what is in season, looks fresh, and is most appealing to the eye. Imagine how each element will taste in combination with the others, and try to balance tart with mild, or spicy with sweet. Choose the most pleasing shapes, and use the color of one ingredient to offset another. The same principles apply when gathering greens and flowers from the out of doors. Don't overlook the tiny violet that could bring life to your salad of sliced fruit and watercress. You might even enjoy a little research. Look in a nature guide to learn to identify what's around you. You may have clusters of redwood sorrel, with its wonderful applelike taste, growing right outside your door. Once you've gathered the salad greens (and yellows, pinks, purples, blues, etc.), improvise using the many flavors, textures, colors, and shapes you have before you. Don't crowd the greens onto the plate; use it as a backdrop for your presentation of color and design. Finally, try planting something! Even if it's just in a deck planter, if you're a city dweller. Yellow pear tomatoes may flourish on your patio. Growing something adds dimension to your salads. It's fun to serve something you've raised, and the process is easier than you'd think. As an inexperienced gardener, I was nervous about planting delicate lettuces. I started a small garden with arugula, and in three weeks, with just water and high hopes, I was serving my own first tender greens. Gradually I added some sucrine, red leaf, and romaine. Some plants I started from seed; others I purchased as seedlings from a garden supply. While my methods may have been unorthodox, and my furrows not perfectly tended, everything grew! I discovered that seeing an edible plant progress through different stages was an education, and there was almost always something to eat. I enjoyed my first radish sprouts. I learned that when the arugula flowered the leaves turned bitter and undesirable, yet there was a profusion of delicate edible blossoms to enjoy. This book is intended to be a resource and an inspiration. I hope you will not only re-create the salads you see here, but also go on to develop your own salad style. Experiment, try new flavors, be on the lookout for special ingredients, improvise, trust your own inspiration, and most of all, enjoy salad.

Amy Nathan

Glossary
of
Greens

Amaranth (Amaranthus)
also Chinese Spinach

Amaranth has had a rather checkered past. Hernando Cortes, the famous explorer, discovered it in Central America, where its leaves were as common and essential to the Indians' diet as corn. According to legend, the seeds were also used in religious ceremonies. They were mixed with blood and molded into idols, then eaten at the end of the ritual. The Spanish promptly outlawed the use of this mysterious plant, and only recently has it enjoyed a revival for its high protein content and delicious, spinachlike flavor.

There are over fifty varieties of amaranths, the most common of which is *A. tricolor.* The plant has slightly rounded green leaves that are sometimes blotched with red.

Amaranth will grow in poor soil; pick it while it is young and tender.

Anise (Pimpinella anisum)

The culinary and medicinal use of anise goes back to its earliest origins in ancient Egypt. Ancient Greeks and Romans used anise in a digestive cake called *mustace,* and it was the Emperor Charlemagne's favorite herb. Anise is still used to give some medicines that distinctive licorice flavor and is still believed to promote digestion.

Anise has bright-green feathery foliage with licorice-flavored leaves, and produces an umbrella-shaped cluster of small whitish flowers. The entire plant can be eaten raw.

Sow anise seeds in early spring in rich, well-drained soil in full sun; keep the soil relatively dry. Pick the young leaves as you need them, but avoid stripping the plant.

Arugula (Eruca sativa)
also Roquette, Rocket, Rugula

Arugula has been a popular green since the salad days of the ancient Romans. It first grew wild throughout the Mediterranean regions, and was gathered for its spicy, delicately peppery flavor. In Europe it has always been a favorite green, particularly in southern Italy and France, where it is an essential ingredient of *mesclun,* the Provençal mixture of tiny salad greens.

Arugula has smooth, small notched leaves of dark green. Related to the mustard family, it has that characteristic tartness, which combines well with milder greens. Eat arugula when it is very young, before the plant flowers and the leaves become tough and bitter.

Despite its long history, seed companies began offering arugula as a "new salad green" a few years ago. It should be grown in cool weather in rich, moist soil, in full sun. Sow in very early spring, or later summer for a fall crop. Harvest the young plant before it reaches 6 inches, or use the outside leaves as you need them.

Basil (Ocimum)

Basil is native to tropical Asia, where Indians worshipped it as a sacred protector against evil. The ancient Greeks and Romans cultivated it for centuries, believing it to have mysterious restorative qualities. But its most romantic association comes from Italy, where it was long considered a love charm.

The best-known varieties of basil are sweet basil *(O. basilicum),* purple or dark-opal basil with deep purple leaves *(O. basilicum),*

French bush basil *(O. minimum)*, and lemon basil *(O. citriodorum)* with its delicate lemony aroma. All varieties have wide oval leaves that are silky and a little creased. Choose a firm bunch that has a characteristic minty, clovelike aroma. Avoid limp, wilted bunches.

Grow from seed or transplant tiny plants in moderately rich soil in late spring. Keep basil lightly moist in full sun or partial shade. Pinch off leaves as you need them; this will also encourage a bushier plant.

Belgian Endive (Cichorium intybus)
also Endive, Witloof Chicory, Chicory (U.K.)

Belgian endive is, in fact, what grows from the root of one kind of chicory plant when it is buried in moist earth and kept in total darkness. Its origin is uncertain, but according to one legend, a Belgian farmer, growing chicory for its root (an important coffee substitute), threw some roots into the loose soil beneath a dark shed and promptly forgot them. When he unearthed the roots some weeks later they had sprouted crisp, pale heads of tightly furled leaves.

Belgian endive is usually harvested at 5 or 6 inches, and is a compact head of long, thin leaves of pale yellow and white, with green tips. The leaves should not be brown or spotted. Endive is crunchy, with a pleasantly bitter flavor that complements milder greens or stands well alone.

Witloof chicory is the leaf plant that produces the roots needed for cultivating Belgian endive. Plant the leaf crop by early summer and leave it until late fall. Dig up the entire plant, cut off the leaves to 1 inch of the root, and "force" it in a cool, dark place, such as a basement or cellar: Plant the root upright in moist soil in an ordinary flower pot with the tops just peeking out. Invert a pot of the same size over the top, blocking out all light. Keep moist and dark for 3 to 4 weeks. Harvest the heads when they are 5 to 6 inches tall. Each root produces one head.

Borage (Borago officinalis)
also Bee Bread, Star Flower

> *Ego Borago gaudia semper ago.*
> "I, Borage, bring always courage."

Borage has always been known as the "herb of courage." It has traditionally been believed that the leaves and flowers of borage invigorate and "make men and women glad and merry, driving away all sadnesse, dulnesse and melancholie," as botanist John Gerarde wrote in *The herball, or general historie of plants* (1597). Borage grows wild in many parts of Europe and England, but is also a popular garden plant for its beautiful cobalt-blue star-shaped flowers (also a favorite of bees).

The leaves of borage taste faintly like cucumber and are a refreshing addition to a salad. They are covered with a fine fuzz and should be picked when small and young, for the leaves on the maturing plant become tough and woolly. The blue borage flowers suggest the flavor of the leaves and have a tiny sweet drop of nectar.

Borage is quite easy to grow and will self-seed from year to year. Grow in sun or partial shade, in moderately poor soil. Give borage plenty of garden space, as it grows rapidly and tends to sprawl. Sow seeds in the garden in April or May. Borage does not transplant well.

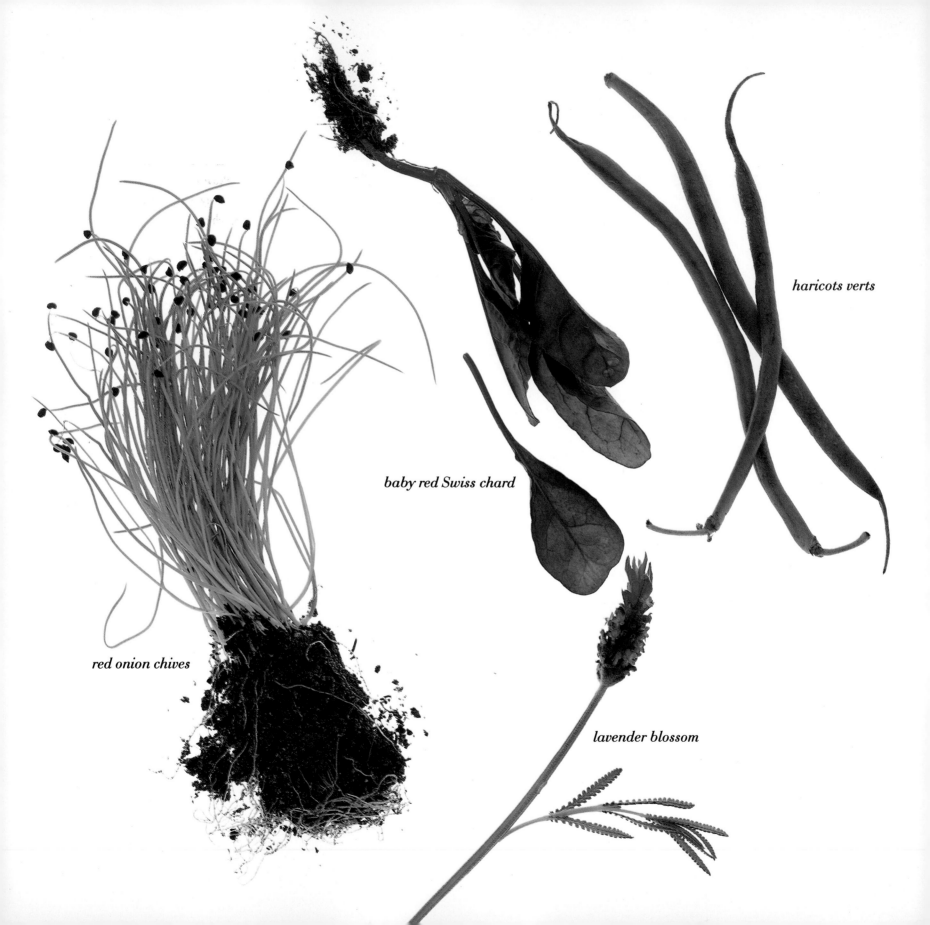

haricots verts

baby red Swiss chard

red onion chives

lavender blossom

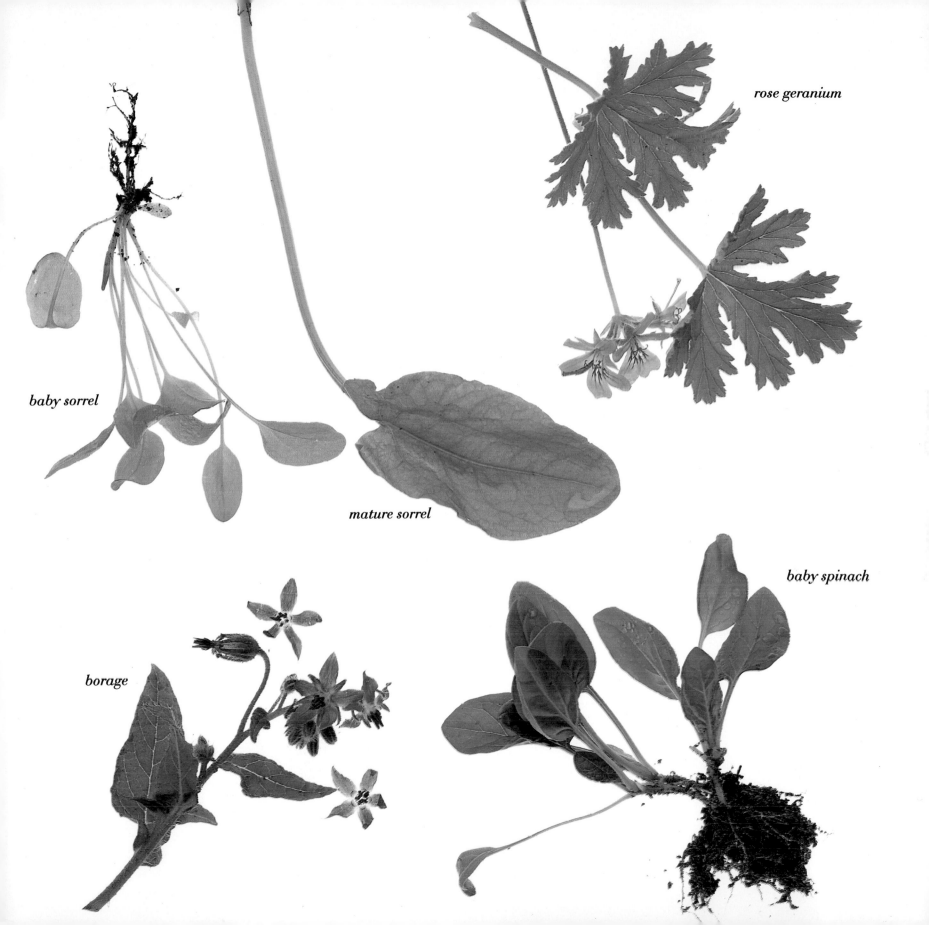

rose geranium

baby sorrel

mature sorrel

baby spinach

borage

Cabbage (Brassica oleracea)

Almost every cuisine in the world includes this richly nutritious vegetable. There are dozens of varieties, the most common of which are green cabbage, with smooth pale-green leaves; red, with deep-red leaves and a compact head; Savoy, which has crinkly pale-green leaves in a long, loose head; Chinese or Napa, with yellowish-green, thick, overlapping leaves; and kale, a looser head with coarse leaves.

Cabbage is an example of a vegetable that suffered when bred for the supermarket. A home-garden cabbage is more tender and flavorful than the large supermarket heads, and there are many more varieties to choose from.

Start plants indoors in early March, and transplant in April in fertile, well-drained soil that is kept evenly moist. Cabbage heads form on the end of long stalks that may need to be supported as the heads become heavier. Harvest when the heads are firm.

Chervil (Anthriscus cerefolium)
also Beaked Parsley, French Parsley

Chervil flourishes in the wild throughout much of southern Europe, where it was traditionally believed to have rejuvenating qualities and a positive effect on the spirits. It is now considered a gourmet substitute for parsley, particularly in France. Chervil is a sweet, aromatic herb with a mildly aniselike flavor and a delicate fernlike foliage that can be used with abandon in salads.

Grow in moderately rich, well-drained soil in partial shade. Chervil self-sows easily, so for more plants the following spring allow the late-summer flower to mature.

Chicory (Cichorium endivia)
also Curly Leaf Endive, Chicorée Frisée

There are dozens of chicories, all with long histories of use in everything from salads to medicine and coffee. The English called it "succory," and Americans have cultivated chicory since the early nineteenth century.

The chicory considered here, also called curly leaf endive, forms a low-growing head of large, curly, frilly-edged leaves. Five seconds of blanching in boiling water will soften its slightly bitter taste, if desired, but it is delicious raw.

Sow in midsummer for a fall crop, keeping the plant moist and fertilized. Use outside leaves as you need them, or harvest the entire plant 1 inch from the base to encourage subsequent crops.

Chives (Allium schoenoprasum)

Chives flourish wild in damp meadows in many parts of the world. They are a hardy onion relative with a delicate onion flavor. Chives grow in dense clumps of hollow, grasslike leaves of deep green that reach up to 10 inches tall. The plants produce a beautiful fuzzy ball-shaped flower of lavender or white, which is edible as well. Garlic chives, as their name indicates, have a mild garlic flavor.

Chives are available in the market during the summer and early fall months, but are relatively easy to grow. They prefer full sun and rich, moist soil. Seeds are slow to germinate, but clumps can be divided every two years for more plants. Snip the leaves close to the bottom to harvest (do not snip the tips only), preferably before the plant flowers (after which you can cut the entire plant down to 3 inches for new, tender sprouts).

Cilantro (Coriandrum sativum)
also Coriander, Chinese Parsley

Cilantro is the distinctive piquancy detectable in so many Mexican and Chinese dishes, and is the characteristic flavor in *ceviche*, a Mexican salad of marinated raw fish. It looks like and is related to parsley, but has a pungent, spicy flavor. Cilantro leaves are thin ovals with deeply serrated edges. Its seed, called coriander, is commonly found in spicy cuisines.

Cilantro is available in many markets, but is will often be labeled as Chinese parsley or coriander.

Like parsley, cilantro is slow to germinate, but a moist, light seed bed promotes growth. Sow every two weeks throughout the growing season for a continuous supply.

Cress (Lepidium)

Cresses grow wild in thick, aromatic clusters of bright-green serrated leaves. Garden cress *(L. sativum),* also called golden or common cress, has fine, textured leaves and a peppery flavor. Winter or upland cress *(Barbarea vulgaris)* has broader, thicker leaves, is a deeper green, and has a less peppery flavor than its counterpart. Nasturtium has sometimes been called Indian cress because of its peppery, cresslike taste, but is not a true cress (see Nasturtium). Watercress actually belongs to the nasturtium family and thrives under very different growing conditions (see Watercress).

Grow all cresses in rich, moist soil, in partial sun. Sow garden cress in early spring and again every several weeks for a continuous supply. Plant winter cress in late summer; it will winter over when mulched and appear in very early spring. Harvest while the weather is still quite cool.

Dandelion (Taraxacum dens-leonis)

This tender green is recognizable to many as one of the more stubborn lawn weeds. But dandelion has lately enjoyed a new appreciation for its rich vitamin and mineral content (particularly iron, of which it has more than almost any other vegetable). The English name probably derives from the French phrase *dent de lion,* "lion's tooth," which describes its long, deeply notched leaf.

Dandelion greens are prized in salads for their tart, slightly bitter flavor. Light blanching removes some of the bitterness, if desired. Some markets offer these greens, but they are simple to grow and even easier to find, though the cultivated variety produces larger, less bitter leaves.

Sow dandelion in late spring in an isolated spot to control spreading. Cut the flower heads before they open to promote more leaf growth. Harvest the small young leaves only, for the leaves of the mature plant become quite bitter.

Dill (Anethum graveolens)

The name for this ancient herb derives from the Norse word *dilla,* meaning "to lull," for it was long believed that dill induced sleep. Dill is one of the oldest-known herbs, recorded in an ancient Egyptian medical papyrus in 3000 B.C. Over its long history it has been thought to cure hiccups, stimulate the appetite, and ward off witches. The Greeks and Romans sprinkled it liberally on their salads, prizing its subtle anise flavor.

rose petals

radicchio

oregano

amaranth

watercress

basil

red basil

mature butter lettuce

blossoming chives

baby butter lettuce

Dill has feathery blue-green foliage that grows up to 4 feet. Tiny yellow flowers in an umbrella-shaped cluster form at the top of tall stems. The seeds and leaves are used in cooking.

Sow dill seeds in rich, well-drained soil in a sunny part of the garden. Water regularly but do not soak the roots. Grow dill near a fence or wall if possible, as the tall, spindly stalks will need to be tied up.

Escarole (Cichorium endivia)
also Broad Leaf Endive, Batavian Endive

Another endive from the chicory family, escarole is similar in flavor to chicory or curly leaf endive. It has broad, flat leaves rather than curly ones, though, and is dark green. Escarole is slightly bitter, and its leaves can be tenderized by blanching in boiling water for 5 seconds.

Escarole is a hardy plant and will winter over if cut down to the base. Plant in full sun in rich, moist soil. Escarole is slow-growing, but the cut-and-come-again technique will often produce a second or third crop.

Fennel (Foeniculum vulgare)
also Finocchio, Florence Fennel, Sweet Fennel

This tall, licorice-flavored plant is rich in history and legend. The Greeks and Romans nibbled it constantly, supposing it to give strength and courage, long life, and good eyesight. They considered it diet food, calling it *marathon* or *maraino*, meaning "to grow thin." It has always been eaten to allay hunger; its seeds were nibbled during the long services in Puritan churches, earning them the nickname "meetin' seeds."

Fennel has a flattened bulb with celerylike ribs and feathery blue-green foliage. The entire plant is edible, but the crunchy bulb has a particularly refreshing flavor similar to anise. Select firm bulbs that are not pulpy or blemished.

Start fennel seed indoors in early spring and transplant outdoors after 4 to 6 weeks. Grow in rich, moist soil and keep well watered. Blanch the small bulbs by piling dirt around the base of the plant. Harvest the entire plant a week or two after the bulb begins to swell.

Fiddlehead Fern (Pteridium aquilium)

Fiddleheads are the very young shoots of ferns that grow in damp, shady woods. Their name describes the graceful curling shape of these tender white fronds.

Do not eat mature fern fronds; search only for the newest growth, which sprouts up in the center of a fern plant. Fiddleheads can be eaten raw and can also be steamed. They have a surprising nutty taste, and an asparaguslike texture.

Flowers, edible

Among the flowers that are edible, small blooms with no hard parts can be eaten whole; otherwise petals can be plucked and sprinkled over salads. Select only flowers that have been grown without pesticides. Flowers should be gathered carefully just before you use them. If gathered in advance, keep them refrigerated in an air-filled, closed plastic bag and refresh by dipping in cold water before using. The important flower rule to remember is to put them in the salad *after* it has been dressed. Your careful selection and care will be wasted if the petals become soaked and heavy with oil.

Not all flowers are edible, but the following make either tasty or attractive additions to salads:

ARUGULA: Once the plant flowers, the leaves become bitter, but the flowers, which are pale lavender or white, are plentiful and tasty.

BORAGE: The blue star-shaped borage flowers taste faintly of cucumber. Remove the fuzzy sepal behind the petals, and use the entire blossom (see Borage).

CALENDULA (also Pot Marigold): Marigolds have been a common garden flower for centuries, and their blossoms have been used in baking, home remedies, salads, seasonings, and so on. There are dozens of varieties, but the most common have orange or yellow flowers. Use small flowers or petals.

CHRYSANTHEMUM: Use young chrysanthemum leaves and petals in salads for a slightly pungent flavor. The flowers should be blanched in boiling water for a second before plucking the petals.

DAY LILY: The edible day lilies are the yellow *Hemerocallis flava* and the orange *Hemerocallis fulva*. Eat whole flowers or petals the day they bloom, but avoid the buds, which have a bitter taste.

Lilies have a slightly sweet and delicate nutlike flavor. Lilies-of-the-valley, however, are poisonous and should be avoided.

GERANIUM: There are dozens of fragrant geranium varieties, including rose, peppermint, lemon, mint, and almond. . . to name only a few. The blooms and particularly the leaves will have the mild aroma and flavor of their namesakes. Geraniums have a wonderful smell and are easy to grow; they are lovely to look at and fun to nibble.

LAVENDER: This Mediterranean shrub produces tiny purplish-blue flowers along tall, spiky stems. Use the flowers and leaves sparingly, as they have a strong lavender flavor.

NASTURTIUM: The colors of nasturtium blossoms are beautiful and various: They range from fiery red to bright yellow or variegated orange. They are as spicy as they look, and taste peppery, like the leaves of the plant. Use the whole flower

as well as the bright-green nasturtium leaves (see Nasturtium).

PANSY (also Johnny-Jump-Up): Though pansies offer little flavor to salads, they make it up in color and texture. Pansies come in every conceivable shade and have a soft, velvety texture. Use the small varieties whole in salads.

ROSE: Roses have a delicate, sweet flavor and add a subtle, pleasant aroma to a salad. The more aromatic the rose, the more flavorful its petal. Avoid commercially sold roses or any others that may have been sprayed with pesticides. Use the petals only.

SCOTCH BROOM: These bright yellow blossoms have a honeylike flavor that becomes more pronounced when the blossoms are dried.

VIOLET: Violets are high in vitamins A and C, and whole flowers, stems, and leaves are edible in salads. The delicate blooms are purple or pink, with a slightly spicy and sweet flavor.

arugula

nasturtium blossoms and leaves

miner's lettuce

chervil

cilantro with blossoms

baby limestone lettuce

baby zucchini

baby carrot

rosemary

Greens

All greens share a tart, slightly bitter flavor and a coarse leaf. Most varieties are from the cabbage family, with two exceptions: beet greens and Swiss chard, both of which are from the beet family. Spinach and dandelion often fall into the "greens" category, but are cultivated under different conditions (see Dandelion, Spinach). Some of the tougher greens benefit from light steaming or sautéing to soften the bitter taste.

Greens grow quickly and will tolerate cold temperatures. Plant the seeds at intervals throughout the spring and summer for a regular supply. Harvest the leaves as you need them, while the plant is young and tender.

BEET GREENS: These greens have a mildly bitter flavor with an earthy aftertaste. The beets themselves are delicious raw, especially when eaten quite young.

MUSTARD GREENS: Mustards have a tart, very pungent flavor ranging from quite mild to hot and peppery. Eat the tender leaves, stalks, and buds raw in salads.

Mustards are very high in vitamins A and B.

RAPE (also Broccoli de Rabe, Salad Rape): This is a leaf plant only, with a mild flavor. It is a favorite salad green in Italy; its leaves, stems, and small bud clusters can be eaten raw.

SWISS CHARD: Chard belongs to the beet family, but its tasty part is above ground. Its coarse leaf is mild and should be eaten when tender.

TURNIP GREENS: Another green from the cabbage family. Turnips produce a tart leaf that is best eaten when very young. The mild turnip root can also be grated raw into salads.

Jerusalem Artichoke (Helianthus tuberosus)
also Sunchoke, Sunroot

This knobby root plant is neither an artichoke nor from Jerusalem. It is actually the tuberous root of a sunflower relative that produces a very tall flowering stalk with yellow blossoms. The name "Jerusalem" is probably a mispronunciation of *girasole*, the Italian word for sunflower. The artichokelike flavor of the raw root explains the second mistake. The tuber is crunchy, with a delicious, delicately sweet quality.

In the market, look for the firmest roots that are not dehydrated or pulpy. Pare away the brown skin and grate the root or slice into salads.

Jerusalem artichokes grow and thrive under almost any condition. Harvest the root after the flowering stalk dies down, and dig up only as needed.

Leeks (Allium porrum)

Leeks are cultivated widely throughout Europe and Britain and are the national plant of Wales. According to legend, Welsh soldiers wore leeks in their hats to distinguish themselves from their Saxon enemies during the war in 640 A.D., which they won. Welsh men still wear leeks on March 1, Saint David's Day, to commemorate their important victory.

Leeks taste like mild onions but are easier to digest. Their texture and flavor are best when young, though most markets sell mature leeks. Baby leeks can sometimes be found in Chinese or specialty markets. Look for firm bases and hardy-looking leaves.

Sow leeks in early spring in rich soil and water well. As the plant grows, continue to mound dirt up around the base to blanch it. Harvest the whole plant in late fall. Leeks become very gritty as they grow, capturing dirt among their layers; they may be sliced in half vertically to rinse out the grit, or washed whole if small.

Lemon Balm (Melissa officinalis)
also Sweet Balm

Melissophyllon, a Greek word, means "beloved by bees." The Romans aptly used this word to label lemon balm. It has an attractive lemon scent, and its leaves taste lemony and refreshing.

Lemon balm grows in sprawling clumps of small round green leaves and spreads almost as rapidly as mint. It will tolerate most soil types, but likes full sun. Pick the young fresh leaves as you need them.

Lemon Verbena (Aloysia triphylla)

Another lemon scented and flavored plant, lemon verbena grows in full bushes that can reach up to 10 feet. Its leaves are smooth pale-green pointed ovals growing in groups of three or four. Use the leaves sparingly in salads.

Lemon verbena will grow in most soil types in full sun. Keep it cut back for a full bush.

Lettuce (Lactuca sativa)

Lettuce is the foundation upon which the salad was created. It is the "salted green" of *herba salata*, the original Roman salad. Caesar Augustus so revered lettuce as a cure-all that he erected a statue in its honor. The Romans introduced it to England where it caught on quickly, and by the sixteenth century, herbalist John Gerarde was recording the basics of a tossed green salad: "Lettuce makes a pleasant salad, served raw with vinegar, oil and a little salt."

Early American settlers brought many lettuce varieties with them, but over time most dropped out of favor. The growth of cities and the need to ship vegetables long distances forced growers to seek a more shipable, pest-resistant, and uniform lettuce with a long shelf life. Iceberg lettuce was the result, and by the 1950s it completely dominated the lettuce section in most markets. Unfortunately, iceberg lacks flavor, and although it is crunchy, it is quite watery and coarse. Many older varieties of lettuce are reappearing in the markets now, enjoying new popularity for their superior taste and texture.

Growing your own lettuces guarantees variety. Grow lettuce in spring in very rich soil with a neutral pH. Water lettuce well or it will take revenge by becoming bitter and bolting, especially if the weather is hot. Give it room, or it will be spindly and slow-growing. Sow at intervals throughout the growing season for a continuous supply of tender green leaves. Some lettuces can be harvested using the cut-and-come-again technique if they are cut near the base. Looseleafs can be gathered leaf by leaf from the outside of the plant, leaving the center growth to expand.

CRISPHEAD (also Iceberg, Cabbagehead): These varieties have large, very tight heads of pale green leaves. They are usually bred for uniformity and slowness to bolt. They have a very high percentage of water and rather bland taste. Their primary advantage is that they stay crisp.

BUTTERHEAD: Of the butterhead varieties, butter lettuce and Bibb lettuce are the most common. They are loose heading, fine-textured heads generally smaller than crispheads. Butter lettuce, also called Boston lettuce, is tender and delicate, with a slight sweetness. The home grower should try Tom Thumb, a miniature head with crumpled leaves, or Trocadero, which has green leaves tinged with red. Bibb lettuce, also known as limestone lettuce, has dark, crisp leaves

red oakleaf lettuce

endive

dill

green leaf lettuce

yellow pear tomatoes

curly endive

red leaf lettuce

fiddlehead fern

tarragon

slightly longer than those of the butter lettuce head. It has a melting texture and an incomparable nutty flavor. Diana, with large leaves, and *Merveille de Quatre Saisons*, which has tender, red-edged leaves, are excellent choices in this category.

COS or ROMAINE LETTUCE: Romaine was originally called Cos lettuce by the Romans, who claimed to have discovered it on the Greek island of Cos. When the Romans brought it north, the English and Europeans called it *Romane* or romaine, after its purveyors.

Romaine commonly has an elongated head of dark-green oval leaves and a crisp, pale-green heart. The best heads are compact, with no brown blemishes or droopy leaves, and have thick, crisp midribs. Romaine has a pungent flavor and stays crisp. Unfortunately, most markets sell a more mature lettuce that lacks the subtle flavor of the young plant. Try Winter Density or red-edged *Rouge d'Hiver;* semi-Cos types such as Sucrine or Little Gem produce smaller, slightly sweeter heads. Rodin, an unusual semi-Cos type, has star-shaped leaves tinted red.

LOOSELEAF: This large lettuce group contains all the lettuces that do not form obvious heads. The most popular and available looseleaf types are red leaf and green leaf lettuce. Both have a sweet, mild flavor and crisp but tender leaves. Red leaf lettuces have ruffly leaves edged in red, while the green leaf lettuces are light green with an even more frilly edge. Black-seeded Simpson is an excellent green looseleaf; Prizehead and Red Salad Bowl are good red leaf lettuces. *Reine des Glaces* is gaining popularity for its unusual serrated leaves and crunchy texture. Another looseleaf variety, Oakleaf, is prized for its deep, rich flavor and dark green oak leaf-shaped leaves.

Lovage (Levisticum officinale)

This herb has a flavor reminiscent of celery, but with a bite that hints of curry. Its leaves and stalks closely resemble celery and are dark green and glossy. Use the spicy leaves sparingly.

Lovage is easy to grow, but is one plant that likes a winter freeze. It dies down each fall and is the first to emerge in early spring. Grow in full sun in rich, moist soil. One plant is plenty; pick the young leaves as you need them.

Mâche (Valerianella locusta)
also Corn Salad, Lamb's Lettuce

Mâche was gathered in the wild long before it was cultivated. European shepherds coined the name "lamb's lettuce" on tasting the tender wild green that their lambs nibbled with such relish. It is also called corn salad, as it commonly appears in fields among corn stubble.

Mâche has small, round leaves of deep green. It has a very mild flavor and a delicate texture. It is excellent combined with the more tart greens.

Grow mâche in cool weather in very rich soil. It loves moisture, does not like being crowded, and hates weeds. Sow in late summer for a fall crop and in late fall for an early spring crop. Pick the leaves before the plant flowers. Harvest the entire plant, or pick only the outer leaves to promote new growth from the center.

Marjoram (Origanum majorana)

This sweet-smelling perennial herb grows with abandon over the hillsides of the Mediterranean countries. The ancient Greeks called it *amarkos*, or "joy of the mountains," and believed it brought peace of mind.

Marjoram is a bushy plant with small rounded gray-green leaves with a velvety texture. It produces clusters of small white flowers. Use the leaves in salads, but be subtle—marjoram has a sweet but pungent taste.

Grow in full sun in well-drained chalky soil. Keep lightly moist, and do not let the soil dry out.

Miner's Lettuce (Claytonia perfoliata)
also Winter Purslane, Claytonia

Miner's lettuce got its name from the miners of Gold Rush days who, hard pressed for edible and nutritious greens in the hills, took culinary advantage of this abundant lettucelike plant growing wild throughout the West.

Miner's lettuce is high in vitamin C and has a delicious mild lettuce flavor and texture. It has pale- to deep-green saucer-shaped leaves on low flowering stalks that grow right through the center of the leaf and sprout tiny white or pink flower clusters. All of the plant above ground is edible.

Miner's lettuce likes partial shade and a good deal of moisture. Plant in late summer for a late fall crop or very early spring for a summer crop. Seeds left in the ground over winter will sprout again in spring.

Mint (Mentha)

No herb is more familiar in taste and smell than mint. It flavors toothpastes, chewing gums, teas, and summer cocktails. Its use is so old and so widespread that its origin cannot be traced, and its years of cultivation have produced over forty flavorful varieties.

Spearmint *(M. viridis)* has light-green, serrated oval leaves with a tart, cool flavor. Peppermint *(M. piperita)* has darker, smoother leaves and an even stronger mint flavor. Pineapple mint *(M. variegata)*, with its green to variegated green and white woolly leaves, has an appealing aroma and a very mild flavor. The gray-green woolly leaves of apple mint *(M. rotundifolia)* have a light apple aroma and flavor. Lemon mint *(M. citrata)* has deep-green glossy leaves with a distinct lemony aroma. Pennyroyal *(M. pulegium)* is a small-leaved creeper that forms a dense, aromatic ground cover.

Mints spread rapidly and will thrive under nearly any condition. They prefer sun, water,

and moderately rich soil, but are definitely *not* fussy.

Nasturtium (Tropaeolum majus)
also Indian Cress

In the succulent nasturtium, the Romans saw a gruesome symbol for the captured armor of their defeated enemies, the "trophy" *(tropaeum)* of battle. Its shield-shaped leaves offset by variegated flowers suggesting a bloodstained golden helmet inspired this martial image. Both the deep-green leaves and the sunset-colored flowers add a refreshing sharp hotness to salads.

Soak nasturtium seeds in water overnight before planting. Sow in mid-spring for a summer-long bed. Grow in full sun in moderately rich, well-drained soil.

Oregano (Origanum vulgare)
also Wild Marjoram

Oregano is often considered marjoram's unruly cousin. Its flavor is similar but a bit sharper, and its leaves are a slightly darker green. Oregano spreads rapidly in trailing clumps. To keep it bushy and tall, snip off the flowering stalks as they appear.

wild onion

redwood sorrel

red cabbage

kale

arugula flowers

radish sprouts

mustard greens

tarragon

Grow in full sun in moist, well-drained soil. Oregano thrives with very little attention.

Parsley (Petroselinum crispum)

Parsley is so rich in vitamins A and C that just one teaspoonful fulfills the minimum daily requirement. But it does more than that. Parsley is said to eliminate garlic and onion odors from the breath, and also to cure baldness!

The most common plant is curly parsley, but a more aromatic variety is flat-leaf or Italian parsley. Select bright-green, crisp-looking bunches with no wilted leaves or yellowed edges.

Parsley seeds germinate extremely slowly (according to ancient folktale, they must travel nine times to the devil before coming up, and he keeps a few for himself each time). To speed germination, soak the seeds in water for 24 hours before planting. Grow in a cool, partially shaded spot in rich, evenly moist soil.

Peppers (Capsicum)

Sweet garden peppers *(C. annum)* and spicy, hot chili peppers *(C. frutescens)* are the most common pepper varieties. Within these two species are hundreds of pepper types, ranging from the blocky or bell green, red, purple, and yellow sweet peppers, to long, skinny, hot *serrano, jalapeño,* and cayenne chili peppers. The widely available green bell pepper is actually an unripe red pepper. As sweet peppers ripen, they become sweeter and more colorful, while chili peppers become hotter as they mature.

Peppers should be firm and heavy, with no soft spots or cracks. To peel peppers, blister the skin over a gas burner or under a broiler until completely black on all sides. Place in a loosely closed paper bag for 15 minutes to steam. Scrape or pare away all charred skin and seed the peppers.

Grow peppers in full sun in warm summer weather. Peppers require a long, fairly hot growing season, so start them early indoors or buy established plants. Keep evenly moist.

Potatoes (Solanum tuberosum)

A potato that remains firm when cooked and is slightly sweet and moist is the best type for salads. New potatoes have a smooth texture and hold together when boiled. Several long-maturing European varieties have the nicest texture and flavor. Some varieties, such as knobby Rose Fir potatoes, have eccentric shapes and a delightful buttery flavor.

Purslane (Portulaca oleracea)

Both green and golden purslane are crunchy but mild salad greens. They have an unusual, mildly sour flavor, and the fleshy stems and spoon-shaped leaves are edible.

Purslane spreads rapidly in a low-growing sprawl. Sow in light, well-drained soil in spring after the last frost for a summer crop, and again in summer for an early fall crop.

Radicchio (Cichorium intybus)
also Red Verona Chicory; Tallarosa

> Se lo guardi, egli é un sorriso;
> Se lo mangi, é un paradiso:
> Il radicchio di Treviso!

> "If you see it, you smile;
> if you eat it, you're in Paradise:
> The radicchio of Treviso!"

Though all chicories in Italy are known as *radicchio*, the variety praised in this provincial Italian ditty and the plant we know as radicchio has a compact head of ruby-red leaves. This red chicory is a much-loved salad "green" in Italy, and is grown primarily in a small region around Verona and Treviso in the foothills of the Dolomites.

Radicchio is gaining popularity in American salads for its unique tangy, slightly bitter flavor as well as its beautiful red color. Although it is still relatively difficult to find, some markets have begun to carry radicchio.

With some radicchios, the first planting season will produce a hearty green plant, which should be either cut back in early fall to encourage the growth of the red head, or forced by planting the roots in a cool, dark place. Other radicchios produce a conical head that turns from green to red as it matures in the cooler weather.

Rosemary (Rosemarinus officinalis)

Ros marinus, or "mist of the sea," was named thus because it was said to flourish near ocean sprays. Dozens of legends have surrounded this beautiful evergreen herb, but it has always been known as a symbol of remembrance. It began as a charm against failing memory, and students in ancient Greece wove it into their hair just before exams. It gradually became a symbol of fidelity, loyalty, and remembrance in love, marriage, and death.

The long thin deep-green leaves have a piny aroma and a spicy, minty flavor. If too dry, rosemary will overpower most salads. Use only fresh leaves, which are sometimes available in sprigs in the markets.

Rosemary is fairly easy to grow. Grow in full sun and light, well-drained soil. Rosemary will survive mild winters; it should be brought indoors during cold winters. A hardy rosemary bush will grow 4 to 5 feet tall.

Sage (Salvia)

Sage, from the Latin *salvia* meaning "healthy," has long been associated with the health and wisdom of the aged. The Greek sages drank sage tea to sharpen and preserve their minds, and in the Middle Ages it was known as "sage the savior" and preserver of youth.

There are hundreds of aromatic sages, but most grow in woody bushes of gray-green leaves with tiny blue flowers. Grow sage in sandy, well-drained soil in full sun. Keep evenly moist, but do not over water.

Salad Burnet (Sanguisorba officinalis)

This cucumber-tasting plant was favored by both Napoleon and Thomas Jefferson. Round serrated leaves grow close to the ground in clumps, and, if allowed, a tall flower stalk will produce deep-red flower heads.

Eat the young, refreshing leaves. Grow in poor, sandy soil and keep relatively dry. Cut the flowering stalks before they bloom to encourage fuller foliage.

Savory (Satureja)

Savory has been cultivated for thousands of years. Virgil grew it for the honey his bees made from its blossoms. Both summer and winter savory have a spicy, peppery flavor and small narrow pointed leaves, though winter savory is slightly more tart.

romaine

flowering watercress

Scotch broom

parsley

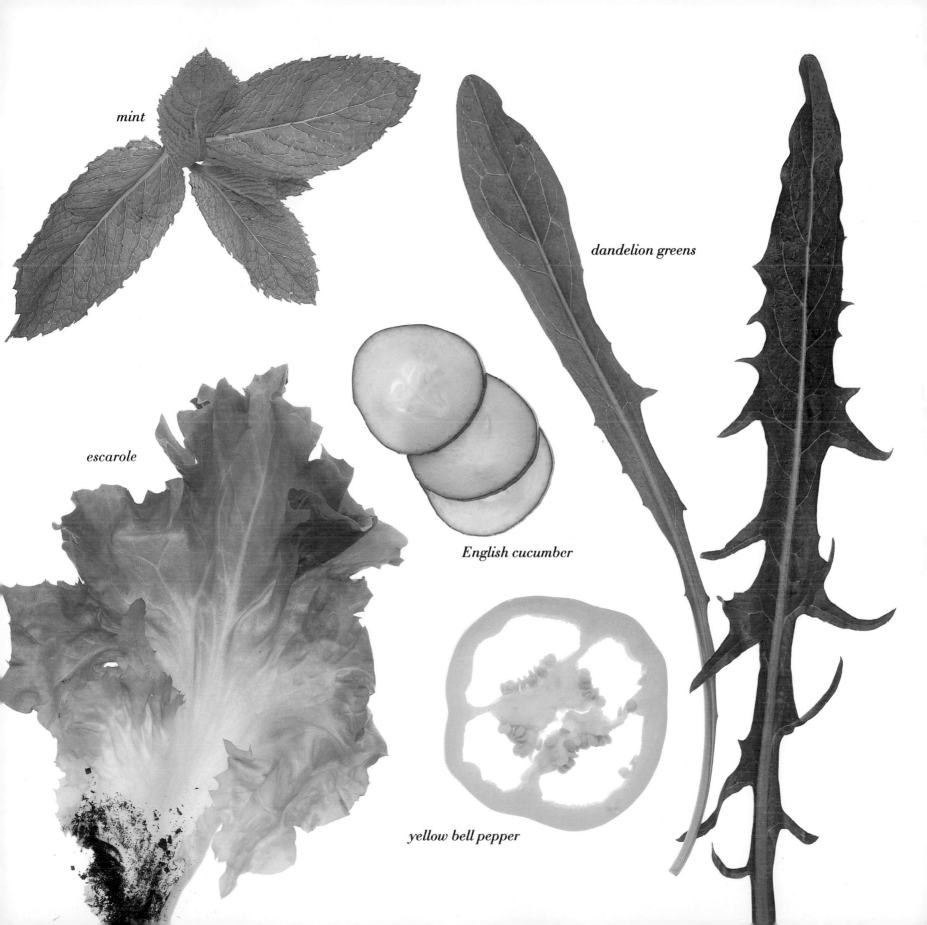

mint

dandelion greens

escarole

English cucumber

yellow bell pepper

Neither variety needs much attention once established. Grow in partial sun in moderately rich, well-drained soil. Allow room for a sprawling plant, and keep the soil moist.

Sorrel (Rumex scutatus)
also French Sorrel

The wild variety of this tart herb is called dock or sourgrass and is distinguished by its sour, lemony bite. Redwood or mountain sorrel, which also grows in the wild, has cloverlike leaves and an apple taste. The cultivated French sorrels have the same characteristic lemony tang, but are milder and have larger, shield-shaped leaves. Sorrel is high in vitamin C, which explains its citrus taste.

Grow sorrel in sun in rich soil. Harvest outside leaves as you need them. Sorrel will self-seed easily, so cut the seed stalks to avoid overspreading and bitter flavor.

Spinach (Spinacia oleracea)

Spinach was virtually unknown in Europe until the sixteenth century, when the Moors introduced it to Spain. It caught on quite rapidly, though, and is now grown in nearly every part of the world.

When buying spinach, avoid wilted or dried-looking bunches. Spinach should have bright-green tender leaves.

Spinach bolts easily if the weather becomes unexpectedly or excessively hot. Sow directly in the garden in early spring (or in late summer for a fall crop) and keep well watered. Harvest the outside leaves or cut the entire plant near the base, leaving the roots buried to encourage subsequent crops.

Spring Onions (Allium cepa)
also Salad Onions, Green Onions, Scallions

Any immature onion can be called a spring onion if pulled while the white bulb is still small. The entire plant is edible, but wilted or dried-out tops should be removed.

Some onion varieties are more suited to cultivation as spring onions. Sow in rich, moist soil in very early spring; harvest when the green tops are 6 to 8 inches tall.

Tarragon (Artemisia dracunculus)

Tarragon established itself early in the European salad garden. John Evelyn, a seventeenth-century botanist, wrote that it "must never be excluded from salletts." It was said to be exhilarating, and one eighteenth-century gardener claimed that the young, tender tops "are very good for Old People. It heats the Liver, and attenuates the Blood." Tarragon has a mild aniselike aroma and flavor, with a slight tartness. Its leaves are long, slender, and deep green, and grow along tall stems.

True French tarragon, the flavorful and aromatic variety, cannot be propagated from seed. If you have seeds, they will produce Russian tarragon, which is a larger but almost bland-tasting plant. Established plants divide into clumps to form new plants, which you can purchase from a nursery or seed company. Plant these in full sun in sandy, well-drained soil. Tarragon spreads easily and should be divided every 3 years.

Thyme (Thymus)

There are over four hundred varieties of this ancient herb, which is symbolic of courage and activity. All thymes grow in bushy, aromatic clumps with woody stems and have tiny gray-green leaves with an earthy, savory flavor. The most common thymes are garden or common, lemon, mother-of-thyme or creeping thyme, and golden thyme.

Thyme can be purchased fresh in some markets, but is easy to grow in your garden or on your windowsill. Grow thyme in full sun in light, well-drained soil. Keep the plant cut back to encourage fuller foliage. It is slow to germinate, but once established will last several years.

Tomatoes (Lycopersicon esculentum)

The Spanish found the tomato in South America in the fifteenth century and introduced it to Europe as an ornamental greenhouse plant. For one hundred years the plants were grown for show only, and the fruits were believed to be poisonous. Finally, the Italians, whose cuisine now abounds with tomatoes, began cooking with the *pomo d'oro*, or "golden apple." Raw tomatoes were not eaten in this country until this century.

There are dozens of tomato varieties, in round, plum, or cherry shapes, on slender, bushy, or dwarf plants. Many round tomato varieties, such as beefsteak or Golden Boy, are excellent raw. Pear tomatoes tend to be low in acid, and are delicious dried (available in Italian delicatessens).

Tomatoes will grow in almost any container, so apartment dwellers can enjoy the sweet flavor of a vine-ripened tomato. Grow in rich, well-drained soil in lots of sun.

Watercress (Nasturtium officinale)

Peppery, nutritious watercress has long served as both a food and a medicine. One Greek proverb claimed: "Eat cress and gain more wit." It grows profusely along streams and springs in limestone-rich areas, but is unfortunately often accompanied with its poisonous look-alike, called fool's cress or marshwort. Be certain you can positively identify watercress before gathering it in the wild.

Watercress has smooth round leaves and crunchy stems that have a distinct peppery bite. It is an excellent salad green, either served alone or combined with milder greens. Watercress is available year round; choose bright, crisp bunches with no yellow or drooping leaves. Store upright in water in the refrigerator, or, rinsed and drained, in a self-sealing plastic bag.

Plant seeds or plants in a shady spot in rich, damp soil, or if possible, alongside moving water. Plants can sometimes be propagated from store-bought watercress; plant stems directly in soil and they may root. Watercress spreads rapidly if grown in proper conditions. Pick the leaves and stems when the plant is young and tender, before it flowers.

Oils
&
Vinegars

Oils

A salad is not complete without its light coat of dressing, whether it be a tart mustard vinaigrette, a creamy curry mint, or simply a thin layer of olive oil. Dressings complement the texture and aroma of the salad, accent its tartness, and bring out subtle flavors. The foundation of a good dressing is the oil. It is the underlying flavor on which the salad rides. The variety in oils makes it possible to select one that is just the right backdrop for your salad.

Olive oil has long been the all-purpose salad oil; its range of flavors makes it quite versatile, and it has been widely available for some time. But many other oils are emerging as excellent, flavorful salad oils, especially the nut oils, which have a rich nutty taste and smooth texture.

Select oils that have been extracted by the cold-press method; heat or chemical extraction gives oil a long shelf life, but it also tends to kill some of its flavor and important nutrients. Cold-pressed oils can be found in gourmet markets or natural foods stores, often in the refrigerated section. Avoid using what are labeled "vegetable oils" in salads. These are blended oils that have little flavor and a lot of additives.

Peanut Oil:
Most peanut oils lack flavor and character, and tend to have a very oily, heavy texture. But a good-quality, cold-pressed peanut oil will have a slightly nutty but still neutral flavor, good for unassertive dressings or mayonnaise.

Safflower Oil:
This light, pale-yellow oil is very high in polyunsaturates (which break down cholesterol), but has little flavor. Combine it with more flavorful oils or use it alone for very mild light dressings.

Sesame Oil:
Light sesame oil, pressed from raw white sesame seeds, is pale yellow and mild. But the dark-brown Chinese variety, pressed from toasted sesame seeds, has a distinct, toasty flavor. It is assertive on salads, so dilute it with a milder oil or use it on equally assertive greens.

Walnut Oil:
Cold-pressed French walnut oil is one of the most luxurious oils available. Its rich smooth walnut flavor accents most greens. It stands up to tart greens, but will not overshadow mild, delicate greens. Walnut oil spoils quickly, so buy it in small quantities and refrigerate it during hot weather.

Almond Oil:
This delicate nut oil has a rich almond flavor. It is difficult to find except in a few gourmet markets. Buy in small quantities to prevent spoiling.

Soybean Oil:
Strong in flavor (but high in polyunsaturates), soybean oil is not a good salad oil unless diluted with a bland oil or used sparingly.

Corn Oil:

Corn oil is bland tasting, but useful when you want very little flavor added to your salad. Look for cold-pressed, 100 percent corn oils. They taste less oily and are better for you.

Grapeseed Oil:

This lightweight, very pale oil is popular in France and Italy. It is a pleasant salad oil and has a nice nutty flavor.

Hazelnut Oil:

The rich nutty flavor of hazelnut oil combines well with mellow-tasting vinegars and tart greens. Hazelnut oil, as do all nut oils, becomes rancid within a few months, so buy small quantities and keep it refrigerated in hot weather.

Sunflower Oil:

Another neutral, pale oil, sunflower oil can be mixed with more robust oils or used for mild dressings.

Olive Oil:

The flavor of a good olive oil is among the most sublime in the world. Unfortunately, many of the olive oils on the market posing as good-quality oils do not have the full-bodied rich aroma and flavor of the carefully produced extra-virgin oils from Italy, France, Spain, and Greece.

The best oils are extracted from hand-picked (therefore unbruised) ripe or partially ripe olives. Ripe black olives produce the sweet, light-golden oils favored in France, and green, semi-ripe olives produce the pale-green oil with a slight sharpness preferred by Italians.

Quality oils are from the first pressing, preferably a "cold pressing," meaning that no heat or water is used on the grinding stones or during the pressing of the pulp. Lesser oils are produced from medium- to low-grade olives, subsequent pressings, or the use of heat or water on hydraulic presses.

In Europe, olive oil producers are required to grade their oil according to acidity; so the mellowest, most flavorful oils will have quite a low acidity and will be labeled "extra virgin." "Virgin" oils have a slightly higher acid content and are produced from lesser-quality olives or subsequent pressings. "Pure" olive oils are refined from the pulp left over from early pressings, which is pressed again with ground skins and pits. Pure oils are the least flavorful, least expensive, and, unfortunately, most common. Many new California olive oils compare quite favorably with the European oils. They are not subject to the same grading system, but are usually labeled "cold-pressed" if they are, and the label may also indicate if they are from first pressings.

Store olive oil in a cool, dark place in a tightly capped glass container for no more than 1 year.

How to Make Herb-Infused Oil

Oils can be flavored with fresh herbs, which is an easy way to perk up a mild-tasting oil. Combine $\frac{1}{4}$ cup of chopped herbs with 2 cups of oil in a jar and cap tightly; let steep 10 days, shaking the jar from time to time. Strain the oil through cheesecloth into a bottle, cap, and store in a dark, cool place. Herbed oil will keep for 2 to 3 months.

Vinegars

Most salad dressings are built on a combination of oil and some acidic element— that tart, pungent flavor that awakens the taste buds and stimulates the appetite. Lemon or lime juice, mustard, yogurt, or soy sauce can provide this element, but the ingredient chosen most often is vinegar, for its wide variety of flavors and range of strengths.

Vin aigre is French for "sour wine." It is the product of the acid fermentation of an alcoholic liquid, most commonly red or white wine. Vinegars are also made from cider, malt, or rice, and can be combined with herbs, fruit, or spices to produce flavored vinegars. The quality of vinegar ranges widely, and there are so many produced today that selecting one may be overwhelming.

Some of the best vinegars, such as the French wine vinegars of Orléans, the balsamics from Modena, Italy, and the sherry vinegars from Spain, can only be found in specialty markets or gourmet food stores. Many tasty varieties, though, such as herb and fruit vinegars, and, for the more adventuresome, wine vinegars, can be produced at home.

Look for vinegars that have been allowed to mature without pasteurization or the addition of chemicals. They should be clear and have bite. The aroma should pleasantly suggest the wine or liquid from which the vinegar was made. Cloudiness is simply evidence of the fermentation process, and can be eliminated (if desired) by straining the vinegar or heating it just to the boiling point and rebottling.

Aceto Balsamico:
Translated as "balsamic vinegar," this mellow, reddish-brown Italian vinegar is named for its pleasing aroma. Sweet wine that has undergone a long aging in small wood barrels produces the famous balsamicos of Modena, Italy, touted for their smooth, rich flavor.

Champagne Vinegar:
Fermented from champagne rather than white wine, this vinegar has a slightly sweet light flavor with a hint of tartness.

Cider Vinegar:
Cider vinegar tastes faintly of apples and has a strong bite. Its flavor is not smooth or refined enough for salads, but it is excellent for making sour chutneys.

White Vinegar:
Distilled from various grains, white vinegar has high acidity good for pickling, but a sharp taste often too strong for salads.

Malt Vinegar:
Malt vinegar is made from grain and cider vinegar. Like cider vinegar, its tart flavor is too strong for salads, but it is well suited for pickling and chutneys.

Flavored Vinegars:
The high-priced flavored vinegars found in gourmet markets can easily be created at home with good-quality white wine vinegar. Make a flavorful vinegar for seafood by steeping chilies, lemon rind, or green peppercorns in a jar of white wine vinegar for 2 weeks. Garlic, honey, and flower petals, or any spice, such as cinnamon, clove, or nutmeg, also create tasty and aromatic variations for dressings.

Fruit Vinegar:
Fruit vinegars are made by infusing fruit in white wine vinegar. They are popular in gourmet markets, but are easily made at home (see How to Make Fruit Vinegar, below).

Herb Vinegar:
Fresh herbs steeped in red or white wine vinegar impart a subtle flavor. These vinegars are widely available, but you can also make your own (see How to Make Herb-Infused Vinegar, below).

Red Wine Vinegar:

Red wine vinegar can be made from any red wine such as burgundy, Zinfandel, Pinot Noir, or simply red table wine. The purest red wine vinegars are imported from Orléans, in the Loire region of France, but many California wineries have begun offering excellent vinegars of all varieties. Red wine vinegar has a sharp, sweet, full-bodied flavor and, if wood-aged, a slightly smoky undertaste. It combines well with olive and nut oils, and boldly complements tangy greens.

Rice Vinegar:

Though Asian cuisines have used rice vinegar for centuries, it has only recently captured the attention of the American palate. Chinese rice vinegar has a sharp, tangy flavor, but Japanese rice vinegar is prized for its smooth, mellow, almost sweet taste. It is excellent on any salad and combines well with sesame oil.

Sherry Vinegar:

The best sherry vinegars come from Spain, where the best sherries happen to come from as well. They are rich and smooth, with a very slight tartness. Long wood-barrel aging gives sherry vinegars a mellow full-bodied flavor that combines well with nut oils.

White Wine Vinegar:

Like red wine vinegar, this vinegar is made from dozens of wine varieties. Such wines as Chardonnay, Sauvignon Blanc, and Riesling are becoming popular vinegar wines for their distinctive flavors. White wine vinegars tend to have a sweeter, cleaner taste than red wine vinegars, and combine well with milder-tasting greens.

How to Make Herb-Infused Fruit and Wine Vinegar

Some of the best vinegars can be created at home from the flavors and wines you like best. Try Zinfandel wine vinegar, raspberry vinegar, or combine basil with white wine vinegar.

Herb-Infused Vinegar:

Combine 1 quart of white wine vinegar with ½ cup of a chopped fresh herb in a nonmetallic container (a stoneware or glass crock with a loose-fitting nonmetallic cover is best). Stir with a wooden spoon to bruise the leaves. Let steep 2 weeks; stir again. After 2 to 3 more weeks, strain through cheesecloth into sterilized glass bottles (select bottles with pottery, plastic, or glass tops, or use cork stoppers). Add a fresh sprig of the herb to the bottle as a "label."

Fruit Vinegar:

Combine 1 quart of white wine vinegar with 2 cups of any soft fruit in a large nonmetallic container (cut larger fruit such as pears into quarters). Stir well with a wooden spoon to bruise the fruit, but do not mash. Cover and let steep 2 days. Heat just to the boiling point, strain through cheesecloth into sterilized bottles.

Wine Vinegar:

Almost any wine will turn to vinegar with the addition of a bacteria that reacts with the alcohol in the wine, turning it to acetic acid. This bacteria is sometimes visible as a cloudy substance in a bottle of unpasteurized vinegar. Two ingredients are required to make wine vinegar: a wine that has not been treated with preservatives, and a bacteria "starter," which can be created by adding a few tablespoons of unpasteurized vinegar per bottle of wine. Combine the wine and the starter in a nonmetallic container (a stoneware crock is best for small amounts, but vinegar barrels or wine kegs are also available). A cloudy film will form on top of the liquid, which indicates that the bacteria is active. Do not stir or disturb the liquid at this time. The vinegar is ready when it has a pleasant aroma and a "vinegary" rather than a "winey" flavor, usually after 4 to 6 weeks. Pour into sterilized bottles and cap the vinegar tightly; this should retard further fermentation. To eliminate the cloudiness (if desired), strain the vinegar through cheesecloth or bring it just to the boiling point and bottle.

Extras

In addition to the wide range of salad greens and the many oils and vinegars that dress them, a pantry of "extras" can enhance and often add unexpected features to salads.

Salt is one of the fundamental seasonings used on greens, but it should always be used in moderation. Sea salt and kosher salt are the highest-quality salts and are naturally iodized. They come coarse or fine; salt grinders are available for grinding coarse grains of salt as needed. Avoid salts with flavor additives such as garlic or onion, as they are often stale or slightly bitter.

Pepper adds spice to salads, and should be freshly ground to capture its full, biting flavor. Pre-ground pepper lacks much of this characteristic pungency. Black peppercorns are the spiciest; white pepper is simply black pepper with the husks removed and is milder and softer to grind. Young peppercorns are green; they are less spicy than mature peppercorns.

Many dried herbs and spices can add interest to salad dressings if used when fresh and aromatic. Avoid using pre-ground herbs and spices, as they lack flavor. Spices can be used to flavor vinegar, but herbed vinegar should be made from fresh sprigs.

Brown and white sesame seeds have a nutty flavor and can be used raw, toasted, or ground over salads.

Capers, the small, peppercorn-sized buds of the caper plant, come pickled in vinegar or packed in salt. They have a sharp, tangy flavor that is a pleasant addition to some salads.

Garlic can be chopped or minced for dressings, used to flavor vinegars, and can be roasted whole and served alongside a creamy *chèvre* and tossed greens.

Nuts of all kinds serve as a rich, flavorful, and high-protein salad accompaniment. The most agreeable nuts to use on salads are walnuts, pine nuts, almonds, pistachios, peanuts, hazelnuts, and pecans. Use nuts either raw or roasted; roast shelled nuts at 350° for 10 minutes, or until brown. Watch them carefully and do not burn.

Soy sauce, often called *shoyu* or *tamari*, is fermented from soybeans and has a rich, salty flavor. Use it in moderation in salad dressings, and remember to avoid any extra salt.

Honey is an excellent sweetener for salad dressings. It dissolves easily and brings out many other flavors in even the subtlest dressings. Use it sparingly, however, as it is sweeter than sugar.

Mustards can be used in addition to or in place of vinegar in salad dressings. The best mustards for dressings are the French mustards from Dijon, which vary widely from hot and tart to mild, but are naturally sweet (no sugar is added) and full flavored. Grainy mustards tend to be milder; they add texture to dressings. Peppercorn mustards also add texture and spiciness. They can be made at home by adding crushed green peppercorns to a smooth Dijon mustard.

There are hundreds of cheeses, and almost any can be served alongside salads for a savory touch. Of particular note are the increasingly available goat cheeses, or *chèvres*, which come in all sizes and shapes and range in flavor from pungent to quite mild. They are generally creamy and slightly tart with some form of crust; avoid dried-out or withered-looking cheeses, for they are old and tend to be overwhelmingly pungent. Another outstanding cheese is the subtle *bufalo* mozzarella, a very fresh Italian cheese made from buffalo milk. This cheese attracts special attention when served with a first-course salad. Hard cheese grated over greens can add punch to a salad but can also overpower some dressings. Blue cheeses such as Roquefort, Stilton, or Maytag Blue are delicious salad accompaniments, but you should use only the freshest cheeses.

Olives are excellent accompaniments to salads because of their tart, salty flavor. They come small or large; black, green, or red; wrinkled or plump; spicy or mild. Avoid canned olives; the best-tasting are sold loose in specialty and ethnic markets. Olive paste, made from olives and oil, is a delicious savory spread that can be served alongside a first-course salad.

Almost any fruit can be used as the focal salad ingredient or as a sweet aftertaste. Fruit can complement the flavor and color of the salad; use only the freshest seasonal fruits, and avoid canned or frozen fruit.

Recipes

Note: Proportions of oil and vinegar may be adjusted according to personal taste. Keep in mind that the strength of vinegar varies from one brand to another.

Balsamic Vinaigrette

½ cup plus 2 tablespoons
  olive oil
⅓ cup balsamic vinegar
1 tablespoon minced shallot
1 teaspoon minced fresh
  marjoram
· *Combine all the ingredients.*
Enough for 4 salads.

Sherry Vinaigrette

½ cup sherry wine vinegar
⅓ cup light olive oil
⅓ cup walnut oil
1 teaspoon chopped shallot
· *Combine all ingredients.*
Enough for 4 salads.

Apricot-Riesling Dressing

2 cups apricot nectar
¼ cup grey riesling wine
  Squeeze of lime
· *In a large, flat, heavy
pan over high heat,
reduce the apricot nectar to
¾ cup, whisking
occasionally to prevent burning.
Chill before adding
the wine and lime.
Enough for 4 salads.*

Orange Vinaigrette

½ cup French olive oil
¼ cup champagne vinegar
3 tablespoons fresh orange juice
2 teaspoons grated orange rind
· *Whisk the ingredients together.*
Enough for 4 salads.

Limantour Vinaigrette

⅔ cup olive oil
2 tablespoons Dijon mustard
⅓ cup champagne vinegar
1 teaspoon fresh lemon juice
¼ teaspoon minced fresh thyme
Dash freshly ground pepper
· *Whisk the oil into the
mustard. Add the vinegar,
lemon juice, and seasonings,
whisking until smooth.
Enough for 4 salads.*

Scented Geranium–Grapefruit Dressing

2 tablespoons grated pink
  grapefruit zest (blanch if
  bitter)
2 tablespoons sweet pink
  grapefruit juice
Juice of ½ lemon
1 tablespoon champagne vinegar
1 teaspoon cider vinegar
3 tender scented geranium
  leaves, minced
Salt to taste
Freshly ground pepper to taste
¼ cup (or more) light,
  mild-tasting olive oil
· *Put all the ingredients
except the oil in a bowl and
whisk briefly. Add the oil
slowly while whisking. Taste
for seasoning and adjust to taste.
Let sit 30 minutes before using
to allow flavors to develop.
A bitter grapefruit will not work.
This dressing will keep for 2
days. Enough for 4 to 6 salads.*

Tahini Dressing

½ cup safflower oil
½ pound soft *tofu*
¼ cup fresh lemon juice
Generous ¼ cup *tahini*
1 garlic clove, minced
1 scallion, chopped
2 tablespoons *tamari*
⅜ cup water
½ teaspoon salt
· *Combine all the ingredients
in a blender or food processor.
Adjust the thickness to your
liking by adding water.
This stores well if covered.
Enough for 8 salads.*

Sunomono Dressing

1 tablespoon sesame seeds,
  toasted and crushed in
  a mortar while warm
¼ cup rice vinegar
2 tablespoons *mirin* (Japanese
  cooking sherry)
2 tablespoons *tamari*
Optional: a few drops of
  sesame oil
· *Combine all the ingredients.*
Enough for 4 salads.

Chutney–Cream Cheese Filling

½ cup mango chutney
4 ounces cream cheese
· *Purée the chutney in a blender or food processor, then add the cream cheese in small lumps. Purée until combined. (Do not overprocess or cream cheese will break down.)*

To fill the nasturtiums, equip a pastry bag with a large open-star tip, fill with chutney–cream cheese mixture, and pipe into the center of blossoms. The filling can also be spooned in with a teaspoon. Makes ½ cup, which will fill about 12 blossoms.

Green Peppercorn Mustard Vinaigrette

4 tablespoons green peppercorn mustard
2 tablespoons hazelnut oil
4 to 5 tablespoons olive oil
1 tablespoon champagne vinegar
Juice of 1 lemon
Dash of nutmeg
· *Whisk the ingredients together.*
Enough for 4 salads.

Mango Vinaigrette

1 ripe mango, peeled, seeded, and cut into chunks
2 tablespoons sesame oil
2 tablespoons rice vinegar
½ teaspoon curry powder
· *Combine all ingredients in blender or food processor; purée until smooth.*
Enough for 4 salads.

Banana–Poppy Seed Dressing

1 cup plain yogurt
2 ripe bananas
1 teaspoon fresh lemon juice
3 tablespoons honey
2 tablespoons poppy seeds
· *Combine all the ingredients in a blender or food processor. Store in a covered container.*
Enough for 4 salads.

Cucumber Ice

3 tablespoons white vinegar
3 tablespoons sugar
1 English cucumber, peeled and seeded (you may reserve a 2-inch slice from the center before halving to slice for garnish)
¼ teaspoon salt
1 teaspoon minced fresh dill
· *Cook the vinegar and sugar in a small saucepan over medium heat until the sugar is dissolved. Cut the cucumber in chunks and purée in a blender or food processor until smooth. Add the sugar/vinegar mixture, salt, and dill. Purée again until mixed well. Pour into shallow pan to freeze until firm but not hard. Break into chunks and purée again, then refreeze 2 to 4 hours until firm enough to scoop. Makes about 3 cups.*

Raspberry Vinaigrette

⅜ cup raspberry vinegar
½ cup light olive oil
· *Whisk the vinegar into the oil.*
Enough for 4 salads.

Pear Vinaigrette

⅜ cup pear vinegar
½ cup walnut oil
· *Whisk the vinegar into the oil.*
Enough for 4 salads.

Creamy Lemon-Pepper Dressing

⅔ cup plain yogurt
1½ tablespoons white wine vinegar
½ tablespoon fresh lemon juice
Salt to taste
Freshly ground black pepper to taste
· *Whisk together all the ingredients.*
Enough for 4 salads.

Thai Vinaigrette I

2 tablespoons hot chili oil
2 tablespoons Oriental sesame oil
¼ cup rice vinegar
Scant ¼ cup *tamari*
· *Whisk the ingredients together; shake before serving.*
Enough for 4 salads.

Thai Vinaigrette II

¼ cup olive oil

2 tablespoons hot chili oil

1 large garlic clove, minced

½ cup rice vinegar

3 tablespoons *tamari*

2 dried red peppers (or to taste)

· *Combine the oils and garlic.*
Whisk in the vinegar and tamari.
Add the peppers. This dressing
will get hotter the longer it
stands.
Enough for 4 salads.

Note: The two Thai Vinaigrettes
are very similar, yet there is
a purpose to their difference.
Thai I is good for fruit and
vegetable salads. Thai II contains
olive oil, which enhances
chicken or meat salads, but
detracts from fruit.

Champagne Vinaigrette

⅜ cup champagne vinegar

½ cup walnut oil

· *Whisk the vinegar into the oil.*
Enough for 4 salads.

Aïoli

4 to 6 garlic cloves

1 egg

1 teaspoon fresh lemon juice

1 teaspoon Dijon mustard

½ teaspoon salt

¼ teaspoon ground white pepper

¾ cup oil, half peanut and half
olive

· *Chop the garlic with a metal*
blade in a food processor. Add
the egg, lemon juice, mustard,
salt, and pepper, and process to
combine. With the machine
running, slowly begin to drip
the oils into the mixture.
Continue to add all the oil in
a fine stream, until it has
the consistency of mayonnaise.

Hazelnut Vinaigrette

⅜ cup champagne vinegar

½ cup hazelnut oil

Dash salt

Freshly ground pepper

· *Whisk the vinegar into the oil.*
Add salt and pepper to taste.
Enough for 4 salads.

Curry-Cream Dressing

1 cup heavy cream

⅔ teaspoon curry powder

4 to 5 large mint leaves, cut into
fine strips

· *Whisk the ingredients together*
lightly. Do not beat. Let stand
in a cool place 15 to 30 minutes
before serving. Reblend
with a fork, or whisk right
before serving.
Enough for 4 salads.

Wild and Gathered Dressing

1½ tablespoons balsamic
vinegar

Juice of ½ lemon

Grated zest of ½ lemon

¼ teaspoon minced garlic

1 small shallot, minced

4 fresh raspberries

Salt to taste

Freshly ground pepper to taste

¼ cup (or more) fruity virgin
olive oil

2 to 4 tablespoons of *pancetta*
drippings

· *Put all the ingredients except*
the oil and drippings in a bowl
and whisk briefly. Add the
drippings and oil slowly
while whisking. Make
sure that the raspberries
are well mashed. Taste for
seasoning and adjust to
taste. Can be strained for
serving or left as is. This
dressing can be used immediately
or will hold for 3 days.
Enough for 4 to 6 salads.

Salads

Barton's Wild Onion Antipasto, see page 119.

Arugula with Packham

Pears and Borage

Blossoms

Dressed with

Pear Vinaigrette.

Nutty arugula and sweet pears make this salad an excellent after-dinner course. Prepare the salad before dinner; a squeeze of lime over the pears will keep them from darkening. Bartlett, Comice, or Bosc pears can be substituted for the Packhams. Select ripe pears that are firm but not mushy.

**Babcock Peaches with
Black Pepper**

**Sliced Babcock peaches
dressed with a squeeze
of lime and fresh
black pepper.
Accompanied with
blueberries nested
in a chiffonnade
of sorrel.**

*The pleasure of this salad is heightened by the patient wait for the delicious but rare Babcock peaches, which make
a cameo appearance in late July for a short four-week season. Serve these sweet peaches and blueberries
as a dessert salad.*

**Barton's Wild and
Gathered Greens**

**The Greens:
Dandelion and mustard,
redwood sorrel, arugula,
green oakleaf lettuce,
fiddlehead ferns, chives,
lovage, and radish
sprouts. Tossed with
Wild and Gathered
Dressing.
The Flowers:
Watercress, arugula,
Scotch broom, and
johnny-jump-ups.
Arranged with
pancetta, sautéed
morels, and a soft-
cooked quail egg.**

*This array of greens and flowers re-creates the beauty of a walk in the woods. It shows how a salad can be a touch
of nature brought indoors.*

Chilled Asparagus Salad

**Blanched and
peeled asparagus,
toasted pine nuts, hard-
cooked quail egg, and
lemon zest, with a
dollop of sweet onion
mustard.**

This salad demonstrates the "less is more" theory that simplicity can be both beautiful and delicious. Asparagus lovers will eat this as finger food. Serve aïoli instead of or in addition to mustard for variety (or try two types of mustard). If you prefer a vinaigrette, serve this salad with Orange Vinaigrette.

Composed Fruit

**Raspberries, sliced
oranges, and star fruit
with Concord grapes,
figs, mint, and wood
violets. Serve with
Banana–Poppy
Seed Dressing.**

*Let the beauty of the fruit you combine dictate the composition of this salad. Use shape, color, texture, and flavor
to determine your own arrangement. An alternate dressing is the Apricot-Riesling Dressing.*

**Cucumber and
Spinach Salad**

**Cucumbers with snow
crab and tobiko caviar,
"totemed" with a log
of steamed spinach.
Sprinkled with white
sesame seeds and
served with
Sunomono Dressing.**

*Two classic Japanese salads are drawn upon here: the pressed spinach is based on goma-e, and the cucumbers
suggest the sunomono salad. It is a cool and savory first-course salad. To form spinach logs: Wash and stem
spinach, place in steamer basket over 1 inch of boiling water, and steam, covered, for 1 to 2 minutes, or until limp.
Cool, squeeze the moisture from the spinach, and press into log shapes. Peel cucumbers, cut in half lengthwise,
seed and slice paper thin. Flake cooked crab over cucumbers, then top with sesame seeds and tobiko (flying
fish roe) if desired.*

Endive and Apple
with Toasted Walnuts

Dressed with
Champagne Vinaigrette.

This salad is a good choice for winter because its ingredients are readily available. The toasted walnuts give the salad a savory dimension. A light squeeze of lemon over the apples will prevent them from browning. Toast the walnuts for 10 minutes at 350°. Cool before adding to the salad.

Future Salad

**Napa cabbage, hijiki
seaweed, and
blackberries, with
a sprinkle of toasted
sesame seeds. Dressed
with Hazelnut
Vinaigrette.**

*Seaweed has been called the "food of the future" for its abundance and its potential as a vitamin and mineral
source. Purchase dehydrated seaweed from health food stores; reconstitute by soaking in warm water for 30 minutes,
drain, and rinse thoroughly. Slice cabbage and seaweed in very thin strips. Raspberries can replace the blackberries
to provide sweetness and color. Think of this as a new type of coleslaw.*

**Greens with
Cucumber Ice**

**Rodin lettuce, dandelion
greens, and Cucumber
Ice, with herb blossoms.
Dressed with Raspberry
Vinaigrette.**

*This is a salad of pleasant contrasts: the mild Rodin butter lettuce plays off the tart dandelion greens; the coolness
of the sorbet is accented by the warmth of the greens; and the ice itself is an interplay of both sweet and sour flavors.
For Cucumber Ice, see page 51.*

Mixed Greens with
Baked Goat Cheese

Arugula, baby romaine,
sucrine, red leaf
lettuce, curly endive,
and radicchio, with
baked goat cheese.
Dressed with
Pear Vinaigrette.

Tender, freshly picked garden greens are the first choice for this hearty salad, but limestone, butter, and green leaf lettuces are good substitutes. Watercress can be added for a crunchy, tangy contrast to milder greens. Select a mild goat cheese, as baking intensifies its flavor. To bake goat cheese: Brush slices with olive oil, coat with white and black sesame seeds, and bake at 350° until soft, approximately 10 to 15 minutes.

**Mixed Greens with
Smoked Salmon
and Two Types
of Cucumber**

**Red and green leaf
lettuces, sucrine,
baby romaine, and
fresh dill; with
smoked salmon,
pickling cucumber
rounds and regular
cucumber "batons."
Tossed with Scented
Geranium–Grapefruit
Dressing.**

The youngest, most tender greens provide the mesclun for a classic combination of flavors, set off by the grapefruit dressing. If you cannot find baby garden greens for this salad, use mild commercial lettuces such as butter, limestone, and red leaf.

Mussels Limantour

**Steamed mussels
over butter lettuce,
red leaf lettuce, and
green oakleaf lettuce,
with celery chevrons,
parsley, and thyme.
Dressed with Limantour
Vinaigrette.**

*Mussels Limantour was "discovered" as an excellent picnic salad at Limantour Beach in Point Reyes, California.
The cooked mussels marinate in the vinaigrette as you hike, and are pleasantly flavored when you arrive at your
picnic spot. Keep the washed lettuces in a separate container, and spoon the mussels over greens just before serving.
To steam mussels: Place cleaned and bearded mussels in a large pot in 1 inch of white wine with chopped garlic.
Steam 8 minutes, covered, shaking the pot once or twice. Run the mussels under cold water, shell, and chill. Keep
in mind that mussels are delicate and should be kept chilled on a warm day.*

New Italian Antipasto

Endive and mâche with

bufalo mozzarella,

sun-dried tomatoes,

and olive paste.

Dressed with

Champagne Vinaigrette

and a sprinkling of

chopped tomato and

red onion.

The flavors that inspired this book are presented here. Combine bits of each flavor on the endive spears and eat as "finger food." The different flavors will mingle without masking each other. This is a savory appetizer or pleasing first course. Use mâche if it is available; if not, watercress is a good substitute.

**Pasta Salad with
Noisettes of Lamb**

**Warm bow-tie pasta
tossed with olive oil
and Parmesan cheese
on a bed of cool Italian
parsley, topped with
lamb, niçoise olives,
and a dash of sherry
wine vinegar.**

*A savory first-course or luncheon salad. The lamb can be prepared ahead and served at room temperature, or warm,
if you prefer. The flavors are rich but not heavy.*

Roasted Pepper Salad

**Pimientos with green
and yellow bell peppers,
sliced and grated
baby carrots, and Bibb
lettuce. Dressed with
Green Peppercorn
Mustard Vinaigrette.**

*This is a perfect late-summer salad when peppers are at their peak. To roast peppers: Hold over a gas burner on a
fork or place under a broiler, and turn until the skin is completely charred and black. Place in a loosely closed paper
bag for 15 minutes to steam; peel away all the charred skin. Halve, seed, and slice into strips. Serve the carrots
either raw or lightly steamed to tenderize. Try the Roasted Pepper Salad as a hearty first course.*

Rose Fir Potato Salad

Rose Fir potato slices

with Black Forest

ham and fresh chervil.

Dressed with Creamy

Lemon-Pepper Dressing.

Finding a new flavor in something as simple as a potato is an exciting discovery. Rose Firs are small, knobby, fingerlike potatoes with a buttery flavor and texture. Boil unpeeled potatoes in lightly salted water for 10 to 15 minutes, then prick with a wooden skewer or toothpick; they should be tender but firm. Rinse under cold water; chill. Dress the salad just before serving, and serve at room temperature.

Rose Petal Salad

**Endive, rose petals, and
toasted pine nuts, with
a chiffonnade of
limestone lettuce.
Dressed with Raspberry
Vinaigrette.**

Rose Petal Salad creates a stunning visual opener to any meal. The tart endive spears, subtly sweet rose petals, and delicate limestone lettuce combine as an appetizing first-course salad, but it can be a delicate after-dinner salad as well. Use only garden roses free of pesticides. Dress the salad just before serving.

**Shrimp with
Melon and Mint**

**Dressed with Curry-
Cream Dressing.**

*This salad can be eaten year round, depending on the melons in season. Shown here are cantaloupe and
honeydew that have been halved, seeded, sliced, and cut into shapes with cookie cutters. The three mints pictured
are peppermint, spearmint, and bee balm. Shell, devein (if desired), and poach the shrimp in water or wine
until opaque; drain and cool. Design your own presentation, using shapes that strike your fancy.*

**Sliced Chicken
and Mangoes
with Nasturtiums**

**Over a chiffonnade
of escarole, with black
sesame seeds. Dressed
with Mango Vinaigrette.**

*This first-course dinner or luncheon entrée salad can be made from cold grilled, poached, or baked chicken.
Gather nasturtiums, wash well, and pat dry. Fill with chutney cream cheese (page 51). Filled blossoms
will last several hours without wilting.*

**Spinach Salad with a
Five-Minute Egg.**

**Spinach leaves, lightly
steamed shiitake
mushrooms and
corn kernels; with
soft-cooked egg,
double-smoked bacon,
and homemade garlic
croutons. Dressed with
warmed Sherry
Vinaigrette.**

*Inspired by a salad served at the New Boonville Hotel, this is a wonderful salad to serve in early spring when
the new spinach appears, the days are cool, and warm food is comforting. To soft-cook the egg: Place in rapidly
boiling salted water and cook for 5 minutes. Remove and rinse under cold water. Peel and serve whole over dressed
greens. Each diner can then enjoy breaking his/her own egg.*

Summer Harvest Salad

**Eggplant, zucchini,
and blossoming
pattypan squash with
baby corn, buckwheat
noodles, and red-skinned
peanuts. Served with
Tahini Dressing in
a butter lettuce leaf.**

Soba noodles are an excellent backdrop for displaying the bounty of a summer garden. Grill or pan-brown the eggplant before serving. The entire cob of baby corn is tender and edible; it can be served raw or lightly steamed. Soba noodles are available in Japanese or specialty markets; cook according to package directions, drain, and cool before serving. This salad is a meal in itself.

Thai Chicken Salad

**Chicken with red and
green onion, ginger,
cilantro, and toasted
sesame seeds. Dressed
with Thai Vinaigrette II.**

*This salad can be eaten like a sandwich, using the romaine leaves as "wrappers." To prepare the chicken salad,
mix together in a bowl meat from 2 chicken breasts, poached, grilled, or sautéed and cut into strips; 1 medium
red onion, chopped; 3 green onions, sliced, including tops; 3 slices ginger, minced; 4 tablespoons cilantro, chopped.
Toss with Thai Vinaigrette II and sprinkle with toasted sesame seeds. You may vary the quantity of any ingredient
according to taste.*

Thai-Style Salad

Carrot and jícama
with butter lettuce
and sliced papaya.
Sprinkled with chopped
peanuts and lime zest
and dressed with
Thai Vinaigrette I.

Those who enjoy the Thai palate will find this a foolproof Thai-style salad. Slice carrot and jícama into fine julienne strips with a Benriner cutter, a mandoline, or by hand. Shrimp chips can be purchased dehydrated in Oriental markets, and will literally puff up when dropped in hot oil. Their pastel colors make them a fun salad accompaniment.

Tomato Sampler

**Italian Roma, garden
beefsteak, and yellow
pear tomatoes with
basil, marjoram, and
fresh black pepper.
Serve plain or with
a good olive oil.**

Serve this summer salad at the peak of the tomato season, when they are at their ripest and sweetest. These three tomato varieties complement each other in color and shape, but other varieties, such as golden round or tiger striped tomatoes, can be used. Another way to vary the sampler is to cut the tomatoes into three different shapes: rounds, wedges, and halves.

Two-Bean Salad

**Yellow garden and Blue
Lake green beans, with
pepper-cured bacon,
pistachio nuts, and
chives. Dressed with
Balsamic Vinaigrette.**

*Any young, tender bean variety can be used in this salad, but if you are lucky enough to find French haricots verts
or baby Blue Lake beans, use them. Steam trimmed beans 2 to 4 minutes and rinse immediately under cold water
to cool and refresh. This is a savory first-course salad.*

**Warm Red Cabbage
Salad**

**Thinly sliced cabbage,
smoked chicken, and
green pumpkin seeds.
Dressed with warmed
Balsamic Vinaigrette.**

*This a perfect winter salad since greens are scarce at that season but cabbage is plentiful. Warm the vinaigrette,
pour about three-fourths of it over the cabbage, and toss quickly (do not overheat the vinegar or sauté the cabbage);
place on plates. Toss the chicken and pumpkin seeds in the remaining vinaigrette and arrange over the cabbage.
Vary the portion sizes for first-course or entrée salads.*

**Watercress and
Kumquats with
Toasted Pine Nuts**

**Dressed with
Champagne
Vinaigrette.**

This is an excellent basic salad that can be prepared quickly, which makes it an indispensable salad for a last-minute meal. Watercress is available year round, washes quickly, and stores well. The watercress and pine nuts alone combine deliciously; this salad is always a crowd pleaser. The kumquats are for color; substitute any seasonal fruit, avocado, or other colorful ingredient.

Appendix

Seed Sources

EAST COAST

W. Atlee Burpee Co.
300 Park Avenue
Warminister, PA 18974
(all outlets have now been
consolidated to PA office)
(215) 674-4900

Thompson & Morgan
P.O. Box 1308
Jackson, NJ 08527
(201) 363-2225

NORTHEAST

Johnny's Selected Seeds
Albion, ME 04910
(207) 437-9294

SOUTH

Kilgore Seed Company
1400 West First
Sanford, FL 32771
(305) 323-6630

George W. Park Seed Co.
P.O. Box 31
Greenwood, SC 29647
(803) 374-3341

MIDWEST

Sunnybrook Farms Nursery
9448 Mayfield Road
Chesterland, OH 44026
(216) 729-7232

NORTHWEST

Nichols Garden Nursery
1190 North Pacific Highway
Albany, OR 97321
(503) 928-9280

WEST

Southern California
Vita Green Farms
217 Escondido
Vista, CA 92083
(619) 724-2163

Northern California
Le Marché Seeds
International
P.O. Box 566
Dixon, CA 95620
(916) 678-4125

Free brochure available,
plus a very in-depth
catalog for $2.

Gardening Tips

A successful salad garden is the result of thoughtful planning and care, and attention to these fundamental steps:

Carefully observe your garden plot over a week's time, recording how many hours of sun it receives each day.

Draw a "floor plan" of your garden, marking the areas of greater or lesser sunlight. According to sunlight requirements, plan where to put each plant variety (keep in mind how much your family can eat).

Prepare the soil and beds. A light, well-drained soil mixed with organic material is generally the best all-purpose garden soil. Test the pH and adjust the soil composition to make it neutral.

Check the planting instructions on your seed packets, and plant according to those guidelines. Keep the soil moist, but not soaked, while the seeds germinate.

When seedlings have two separate leaves, thin them, leaving plenty of space between remaining plants. *Be sure to thin adequately.* Crowded plants are weaker and quicker to bolt, and they attract pests. Lettuces will be bitter if crowded, and some tend to rot when touching neighbor plants. Sow more seeds every few weeks throughout the growing season for a continuous supply of young, tender greens.

Keep plants watered. Most plants hate uneven waterings, and some will become bitter or bolt if too dry. Morning is the best time to water; moisture clinging to leaves overnight may cause rot.

Be on the lookout for pests and disease; keep them in check before they take over. Weed or mulch to discourage weed growth.

Remember to enjoy your garden! Harvest plants when they are ready, and eat the delicious, fresh greens and vegetables you have labored for. Don't let your garden get overgrown or run to seed.

Gardening Terms

ANNUAL:
A plant whose entire growth cycle spans less than 12 months.

BLANCH:
To whiten plants by excluding all light.

BOLT:
Premature flowering, often due to unusually hot weather or unsatisfactory growing conditions.

BROADCAST:
To scatter seeds randomly rather than planting in rows.

CUT-AND-COME-AGAIN:
To harvest plants more than once during a season to encourage subsequent crops. Cut the plant near its base, leaving 1 inch above ground, then mulch. New growth should appear within a few weeks.

FERTILIZER:
A soil supplement, preferably consisting of organic matter such as manure, peat moss, or compost.

FORCE:
To encourage the rate of growth or to bring a plant to maturity out of its normal season, usually by altering growing conditions.

MULCH:
A protective layering of material (such as sawdust, manure, grass clippings, compost, or bark) to keep in moisture, discourage weeds, or enrich the soil.

PESTS:
Any insects that may attack plants, such as aphids, slugs, snails, cutworms, or whiteflies. Consult your local garden center or specialist gardening book for specific treatment. In all cases, avoid using chemical sprays.

PERENNIAL:
A plant whose life cycle continues for more than two years.

pH:
The scale measuring soil alkalinity and acidity; 1 equals most acid, 7 is neutral, and 14 is most alkaline. Alkaline soil has a high calcium or lime content and can be corrected with sulphur or aluminum sulphate. Acid soil can be corrected with ground limestone.

PINCH:
To encourage the growth of fuller foliage by snipping out flower stalks.

SELF-SOW:
Plants that seed themselves from one season to the next when allowed to flower.

Salad Hints:

Washing, Storing, Dressing, & Serving Fresh Greens

Gather or buy greens just before you plan to eat them, if possible. To wash greens, fill a sink or large bowl with cool water and gently dunk loose leaves or entire small heads several times to loosen dirt. Allow a minute for the dirt to filter to the bottom, then carefully remove the greens to a colander to drain or to a salad basket or spinner. Take care not to bruise the leaves by overcrowding. Greens should be as dry as possible; moisture on the leaves prevents oil from coating them.

If you need to store washed greens, wrap the base of the washed heads or leaves in a paper towel to draw out excess moisture and place in a self-sealing plastic bag. Seal and refrigerate until needed. If you are storing the greens until the following day, remove the paper towel when it has fully absorbed the moisture, reseal the bag, and refrigerate.

There are two schools of thought regarding the proper method of dressing a salad. Some believe the best way is to toss the greens just before serving to ensure that each leaf is coated with dressing. I find that this is true for certain salads, such as cabbage or spinach salads, but that many composed salads benefit from drizzling the dressing over the composition. This requires that the salad be served on a shallow plate, so that all the leaves are coated.

Bibliography

Coats, Alice M. Flowers and Their Histories. New York: McGraw-Hill Book Co., 1971.

The Editors of Time-Life Books. Salads. Alexandria, Virginia: Time-Life Books, 1980.

Ferrary, Jeannette. "It's a Toss-Up." San Francisco Focus, May 1984, pp. 60–62.

Freiman, Jane Salzfass. "Olive Oil." Cuisine, February 1984, pp. 32–34.

Gibbons, Barbara. Salad for All Seasons. New York: Macmillan Publishing Co., 1982.

Harrington, Geri. The Salad Book: From Seed to Salad Bowl. New York: Antheneum, 1977.

Hersey, Jean. Cooking with Herbs. New York: Charles Scribner's Sons, 1972.

Hodgson, Moira. The New York Times Gourmet Shopper. New York: Times Books, 1983.

Larkcom, Joy, in cooperation with the New York Botanical Garden Institute of Urban Horticulture. The Salad Garden. New York: The Viking Press, 1984.

Moment, Barbara Chipman. The Salad Green Gardener. Boston: Houghton Mifflin Co., 1977.

Morash, Marian. The Victory Garden Cookbook. New York: Alfred A. Knopf, 1982.

Nyerges, Christopher. Wild Greens and Salads. Harrisburg, Pennsylvania: Stackpole Books, 1982.

Ortho Editorial Staff and McNair, James K., The World of Herbs and Spices. San Francisco: Ortho Books, 1978.

Ortho Editorial Staff and Scheer, Cynthia, The Complete Book of Salads. San Francisco: Ortho Books, 1981.

Proulx, E.A. "Belle Lettuce." Horticulture, August 1983, pp. 35–44.

———. "Chicory and Endive: A Cultivated Taste." Horticulture, December 1983, pp. 13–18.

———. "The Forgotten Art of Building A Garden of Small Salads." Horticulture, January 1984, pp. 12–19.

Willan, Anne. French Regional Cooking. New York: William Morrow Co., 1981.

Witty, Helen, Wolf, Burton, and Beard, James. The Garden to Table Cookbook. New York: McGraw-Hill Book Co., 1976.

Index

Barton's Wild-Onion Antipasto: (from page 55) *Wild onions, roasted garlic, goat cheese, figs, and niçoise olives, with fresh croutons, rosemary toasted walnuts, lobelia blossoms, and savory. Served with a light virgin olive oil.*

Wild onion is the focus of this savory first-course salad. Wild onions appear in California in January through March; elsewhere they sprout up in early spring. The entire plant, from bulb to blossom, is edible. To toast walnuts: Coat lightly with virgin olive oil and minced fresh rosemary; roast at 250° for 20 minutes.